Vikings Sticker Book

Illustrated by Paul Nicholls

Designed by Non Taylor

Written by Fiona Watt

Historical Consultant: Dr. Anne Millard

Contents

On the farm

People often think of the Vikings as brutal, axe-wielding raiders, but most were peaceful farmers. When the long, cold winter was over they would be busy looking after their animals, and planting crops and vegetables.

Use the stickers to fill the pages with people sowing seeds and feeding the animals. Add the chieftain returning from a hunting trip with his dogs and his servant.

At home

Inside the longhouse it's dark, smoky and smelly.
There are no windows, so the only light inside comes
from the fire and oil burning in small clay lamps.

Press on the stickers of the women busy cooking,
sewing and spinning. Then, add the men lounging
on the sleeping benches at the side of the room.

Sea people

Two strong men are lowering a boy down a cliff to collect birds' eggs to eat, while fishermen are bringing their catch ashore to be dried and stored.

Fill the scene with the fishermen, someone gathering mussels from rocks, women gutting fish and mending a net, along with the seal hunters.

What to wear

It's a warm day so people have discarded their thick fur cloaks and hats. Ladies are dressed in long dresses and tunics made from wool and linen. The children are wearing mini versions of their parents' clothes and foreign merchants, trading cloth, jewels and slaves, are in their fine exotic robes.

Fill the market place with stickers, including a nobleman and his family, someone selling a cow, and some unhappy slaves.

Life in a town

Smoke is rising from houses and workshops, the wooden walkways are bustling with tradesmen carrying their goods, while craftsmen are hard at work making tools and weapons, leather shoes and clay pots. Some people are wearing skates to get about on the icy river.

Scatter the stickers around the busy town.

A feast

A rich chieftain is holding a feast for his family and friends, who are dressed in their finest clothes. Lots of splendid food has been laid upon the table and the guests are being entertained by musicians, acrobats and a poet.

Use the stickers to fill the scene with guests, food and entertainers.

Sacred grove

Sunlight filters through the trees as people gather to pray to their gods. They've brought food, animals and trinkets to offer to the gods.

Press on the stickers of the worshippers who are seeking help in their everyday lives and protection from evil.

Gods and goddesses

The Vikings believed in many gods and goddesses. Each one was in charge of a different part of people's lives. They thought that the gods lived in a magnificent place called Asgard and the only way to reach it was across a rainbow bridge.

Press on the stickers of the gods and goddesses next to their descriptions.

Freya

- goddess of beauty and love, twin sister of Frey
- has magical powers and could predict the future
- rides in a chariot pulled by two great cats

Thor

- son of Odin, god of law and order, storms and winds
- races through the skies on a chariot whose wheels make the sound of thunder
- short-tempered and controls his enemies with his strength and a magic hammer called Mjollnir

Frey

- twin brother of Freya
- makes the sun shine, the rain fall and crops grow
- his symbol is a boar

Hel

- goddess of the underworld
- enemy of the gods, banished to of the land of the dead
- a beautiful woman from the waist up, but from the waist down has the body of a skeleton

Heimdall

- watchman of the gods, guardian of the rainbow bridge
- has incredible vision and exceptional hearing
- warns the gods if strangers approach

The Norns

- goddesses who spin or weave the fate of people
- three sisters, known as Past, Present and Future
- control the destinies of humans and gods
- live beside a sacred well in Asgard

Odin

• king of the gods and ruler of all things, god of wars, poetry and wisdom

• sacrificed one of his eyes to gain the gift of knowledge and wisdom

• has a magical eight-legged horse and is accompanied by two ravens who fly around the world and bring back interesting news

The Valkyries

• fearless, frightening female warriors

• hover in the sky over battlefields and decide who will die

• carry the souls of warriors who died bravely to Valhalla, Odin's hall in Asgard

Frigg

• wife of Odin, queen of the gods

• mother goddess who cares for women, children and the home

• the only person other than Odin allowed to sit on his throne

Loki

• not a true god but lives in Asgard

• loves adventures, mischief and trickery

• has the ability to change shape to become any creature

Tyr

• god of war and the sky

• bravest of all gods, worshipped by warriors

• lost one hand while fighting a giant wolf

Balder

• god of light and joy

• son of Odin and Frigg

• handsome, kind and wise

• loved by both gods and humans

15

A Thing

Farmers and their families have gathered together for an open-air meeting called a Thing. They do this every two years or so. They are discussing local problems, settling arguments and deciding how to punish a criminal. They're also meeting friends, catching up on news and even arranging marriages.

Fill the pages with people surrounding a man who's pleading his innocence. Add old friends gossiping, too.

Trading camp

As the sun sets over the hills, a group of weary traders have set up a camp. They have sailed across seas, rowed along rivers and even 'carried' their boat across land from one river to the next. They've brought furs, weapons, pottery and necklaces to sell.

Press on the stickers of the traders, their goods and the local merchants.

New lands

Good land for farming has been hard to find so these families have sailed west in search of a new place to live. Several weeks ago they loaded their ship with chests, baskets, barrels, food, tools, pots, jugs and even their animals – everything they needed for the voyage and building a new life.

Fill the beach with settlers carrying belongings and leading their animals.

Raiders!

"Quick... flee... run... hide!" Viking raiders, armed with axes and swords, are attacking a monastery. They've beached their longships and are in search of precious treasures and prisoners that they can take home to sell as slaves.

Press on the stickers of the raiders and the terrified monks and farmers.

A burial

A Viking queen has died and she's being buried in a ship with all the things she will need for sailing off to the next world, including her servant girl and her pets.

Fill the boat with her possesions and add the people mourning her death.

On the farm